DRAFT
5/2499

SAMPLING MARBLED MURRELETS AT SEA:
TESTS OF SURVEY METHODS AND DESIGNS

Martin G. Raphael, Diane M. Evans, and Randall J. Wilk
USFS Pacific Northwest Research Station
Olympia, Washington

Introduction

The marbled murrelet (*Brachyramphus marmoratus*) is a small, nondescript seabird that was federally listed as threatened under the Endangered Species Act in 1992. This species has a unique natural history among seabirds in that it travels up to 50 mi inland away from the ocean to establish nest sites in the canopies of large trees in older-successional forests (Hamer and Nelson 1995). Because of its association with late-successional forest habitats, the marbled murrelet became a focal species of the Northwest Forest Plan (NWFP; USDA/USDI 1994), a multi-agency initiative that provided management direction to maintain and restore populations and habitat of late-successional and old-growth species on federal lands in western Washington, Oregon, and northern California One of the critical components of the NWFP and of the USFWS's Recovery Plan for the marbled murrelet (U.S. Fish and Wildlife Service 1997) is the ability to accurately assess the status of the population and to monitor population trends over time. Most of the typical demographic indices used for wildlife species, such as reproductive success, juvenile and adult survival, and longevity, are extremely difficult to obtain for marbled murrelets. Active nests are widely dispersed and difficult to locate due to the murrelet's secretive nesting behavior (Hamer and Nelson 1995, Nelson and Hamer 1995). Mark-recapture techniques refined in the last 3-4 years may lead to refined survival estimates (Cook et al. 1998) but still have limited utility in locating nests. Thus, researchers and managers have concurred that the most appropriate approach to population monitoring is to track changes at sea (U.S. Fish and Wildlife Service 1997, Madsen et al. 1997).

Within the NWFP area, marine surveys for murrelets were conducted by at least five different groups during 1990-97. The size of vessels, number of observers, type and configuration of transect used, and the data collected differed among these groups, yet the extent to which these differences affected the population parameters ultimately reported have not been tested. The Effectiveness Monitoring Plan for the marbled murrelet (Madsen et al. 1997) specified that monitoring under this program would be conducted using consistent methodology (a protocol) throughout the NWFP area. Before this protocol could be defined, a thorough examination of the different methods and an assessment of which techniques best achieved population estimates and indices of productivity was needed.

Marbled murrelets are counted on the water from boats by scanning the area ahead and to the side of the moving vessel. The biggest differences in the methods currently employed are (1) whether data are collected as a strip or line transect (see Buckland et al. 1993); (2) if collected as a line transect, whether the distance of the target from the line is determined by a direct estimate of perpendicular distance or a calculation of perpendicular distance from a direct estimate of radial distance and a measure of the angle of the target from the line; (3) whether a single or two observers are used; and (4) how the productivity index (the ratio of juveniles to adults) is calculated (Raphael and Evans 1997). We tested several aspects of marine survey methods during the breeding seasons of 1997 and 98. Our objectives were to:

(1) determine if density estimates differed when using one vs. two observers,
(2) assess observer variability and accuracy in estimating perpendicular and radial distances,
(3) determine if density estimates differed between perpendicular- or radial-distance based calculations,
(4) assess observer variability in identifying adult and juvenile murrelets,
(5) determine if the spatial distribution of adult murrelets differed from juveniles and if the ability to detect adults differed from that of juveniles, such that productivity indices were affected,
(6) compare age ratios calculated with three different approaches, and
(7) investigate the effect of transect configuration (straight line vs. other configurations) on density estimates.

Results from these investigations will be incorporated into development of the survey protocol for the NWFP Effectiveness Monitoring Program.

General Methods

Our study was conducted in the inland waters of Puget Sound, WA, including Hood Canal (HC) along the eastern side of the Olympic Peninsula and the inter-island passages of the San Juan Island (SJI) archipelago. Observers were positioned in the bow of a 17-ft Boston Whaler equipped with 90-hp outboard motor. This placed observer height at approximately 2 m above the surface of the water. Observers were experienced in estimating perpendicular distances and identifying seabirds. Distance estimates were visually recalibrated each day by deploying a line behind the boat at various distances from 0-100 m. The line was marked with knots every 5 m and with buoys every 25 m. With few exceptions, experiments were conducted at Beaufort sea state ≤ 2. Given that the specific methods for each experiment differed, the remainder of the methods and results are presented by experiment.

One versus Two Observers

Methods.---Data were collected while conducting a 'typical' extensive survey in the SJI. Line transects were run parallel to shore at a 300-m distance. Observers estimated the perpendicular distance from the transect line of all seabirds encountered within 200 m either side of the boat. Observer behavior was standard for line transects: observers focused more effort within shallow angles in front of the boat, but continued to scan out to the sides. Data were recorded into a handheld micro cassette recorder. A transect or group of transects was run first with one observer, then repeated shortly after or the next day with two observers. One observer covered the entire 180^0 scanning window; two observers split the scanning window to each cover from the bow to 90^0 to one side. A total of 9 transects ranging 4-22 km in length were repeated in each of three time intervals beginning in mid-July 1998.

Because it was logistically difficult to design an experiment that provided simultaneous observations of one and two observers, the basis of comparison was the density estimate derived from the program DISTANCE (Buckland et al. 1993) for the transects as a group for each time interval. We categorized perpendicular distances from the line into 6 classes: 0-25 m, 25-50 m, 50-75 m, 75-100 m, 100-150 m, 150-200 m. We expected that birds moved around from the time a transect was run with one observer to when the same ground was covered with two observers (maximum of 24 hours later), but we assumed that the overall population sampled remained constant across the transects within the time interval. However, in an attempt to reduce the added variability from nonsynchronous observations, we analyzed the data two ways: including just the transects that were covered on the same day with one and two observers, and including all transects. Seven transects were run on the same day in interval 1 (mid July), 3 in interval 2 (early August), and 9 in interval 3 (mid August). Note that 'same day' does not mean that the 7 transects in interval 1 were run on the same calendar day, but rather that a given transect was covered by one observer and two observers on the same day. Covering all 9 transects within a time interval spanned several calendar days.

We also compared the number of murrelets observed per transect by one observer compared to two observers with a paired *t*-test, using transects as the samples.

Results.---Density across transects was higher or lower with one observer depending on the time interval and the subset of transects considered (same day or all). When transects run on the same day were considered, there was no difference in density estimates in mid July, one observer had a higher density than two observers in early August, and two observers had a higher density than one observer in late August (Figure 1). When all transects were considered, there was again no difference in mid July, and two observers had a higher density estimate than one observer for early and mid August (Figure 1). Density estimates from the DISTANCE program are most influenced by the number of birds recorded closer to the transect line. The patterns in density estimates reported above were driven by the number of murrelets recorded 0-25 m and 25-50 m from the line. When all transects were considered, two observers recorded significantly more murrelets ($X^2 > 3.8$, $p < 0.05$ in all cases) 0-50 m from the line than one observer in late August, although not in the other intervals (Figure 2). When only transects run on the same day were considered, one observer recorded significantly more murrelets close to the line than two observers in interval 2, and the reverse was true in interval 3 (Figure 3). Combining all 3 intervals, two observers recorded significantly more murrelets than one observer only when all transects were considered (Figure 4). One observer generally recorded significantly more murrelets than two observers at distances > 100 m from the line (Figures 2, 3, and 4).

Results of paired *t*-tests showed no significant differences in the number of murrelets seen per transect per number of observers. One observer recorded, on average, 3 fewer murrelets per transect than two observers when transects run on the same day were considered ($t = -0.378$, $p = 0.71$), and 6 fewer murrelets on average when all transects were considered ($t = -0.84$, $p = 0.41$; Table 1).

Discussion.--Due to the lack of simultaneous observations, this experiment was limited in its ability to assess the consequences of using one vs. two observers to conduct murrelet surveys. Because the absolute number and spatial distribution of murrelets at any one site is in flux, density estimates will vary at an unknown magnitude within relatively short periods of time. Our assumption that murrelets might move within and between transects but that the overall population across transects would remain constant within a time interval is questionable. Our sample transects did not cover all probable areas to which murrelets could move to or from. While we had circumstances under which two observers outperformed one observer (as might be expected), the reverse also was true. Thus, these results do not provide a definitive answer to this aspect of survey methodology.

Our 'typical' extensive survey enlists a single observer but the driver serves as a backup and points out birds that might be missed by the observer. Thus, our 'one observer' sample may more accurately reflect 1.25 observers.

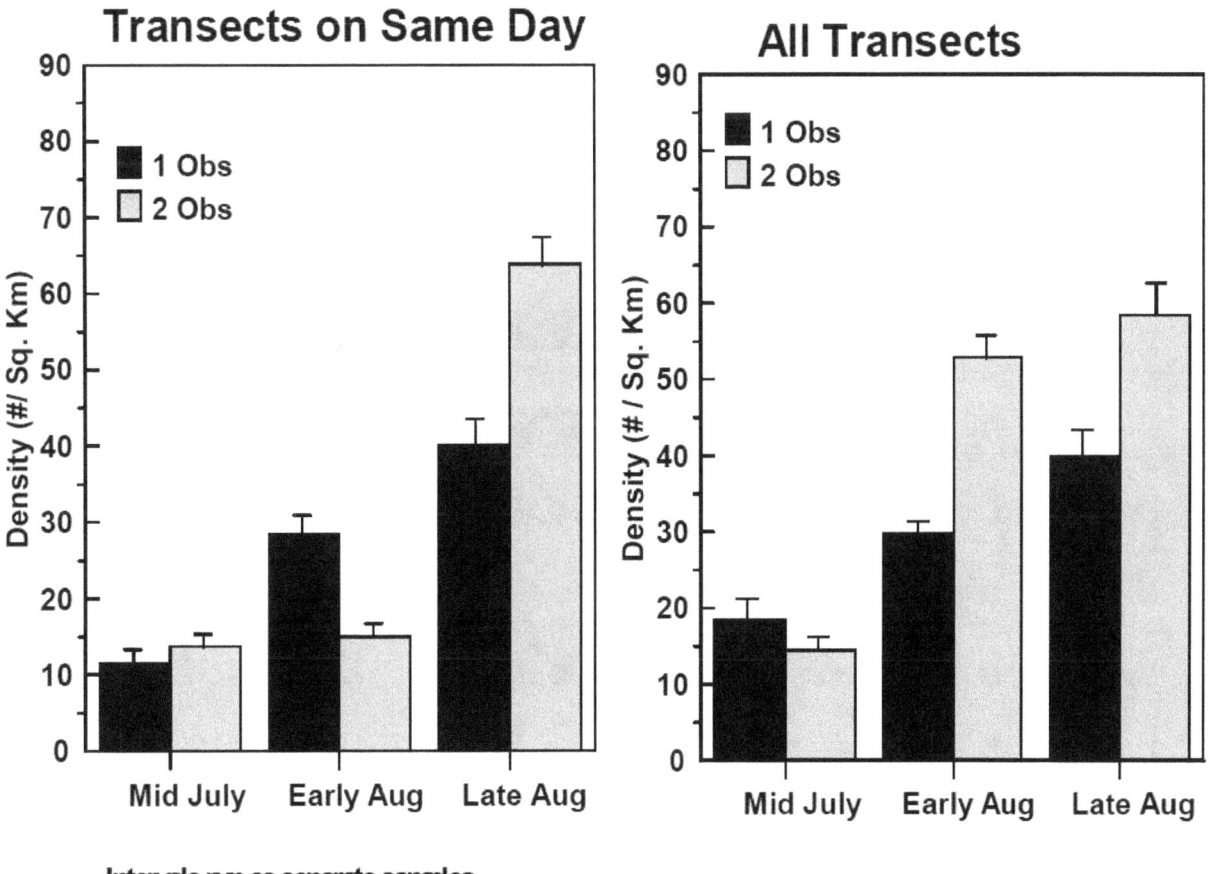

Figure 1. Comparison of density estimates (from program DISTANCE) obtained by one and two observers. 'Transects on same day' refers to the sample of transects covered by one and two observers on the same day (n = 7 in mid July, n = 3 in early Aug, and n = 9 in mid August). 'All transects' includes those run on the same or one day apart (n = 9 in each interval).

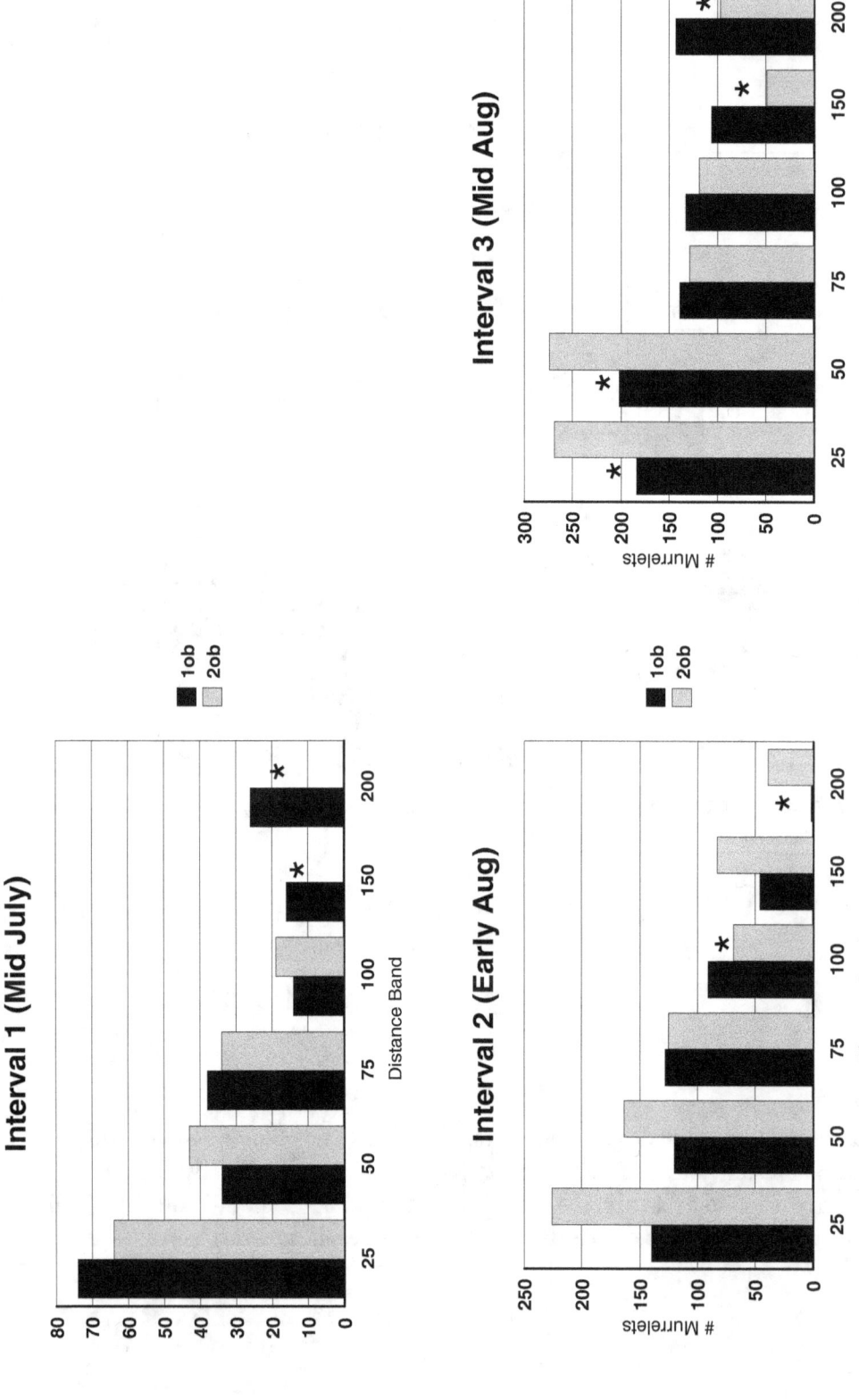

Figure 2. Number of murrelets recorded by distance from the transect line from all transects (run on same or next day). Significant differences noted with '*'.

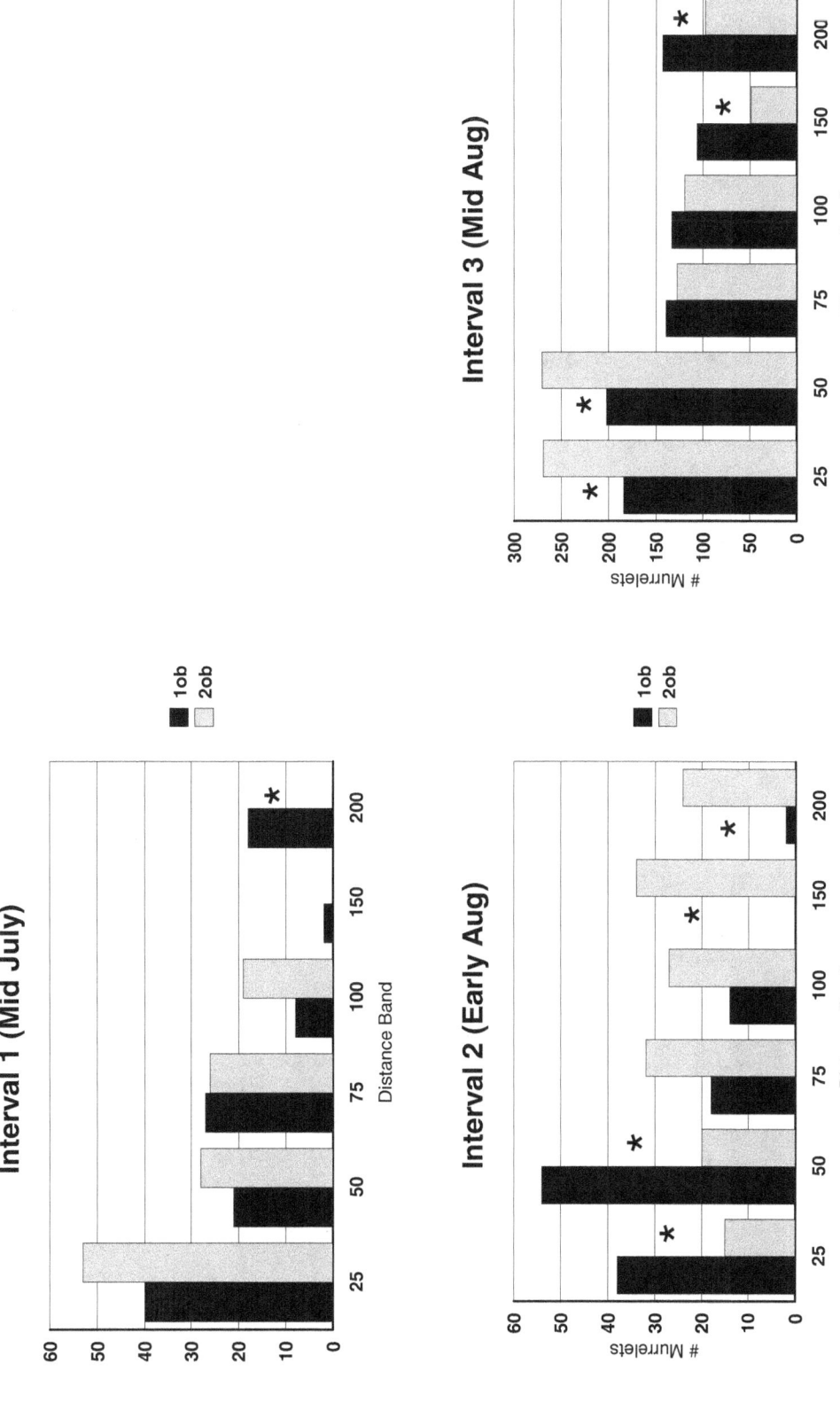

Figure 3. Number of murrelets recorded by distance from the transect line from transects run by one observer on the same day as with two observers. Significant differences noted with '*'.

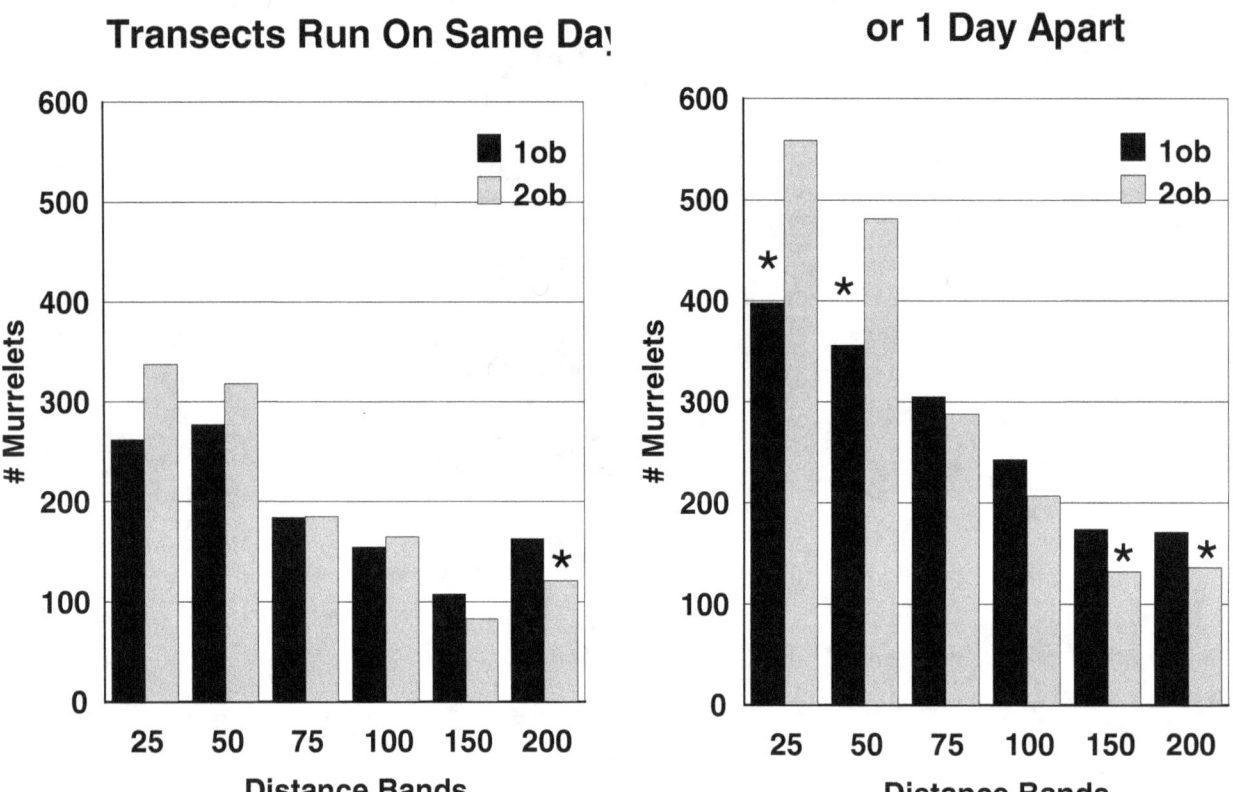

Figure 4. Distribution of murrelets from the transect line pooled across three time intervals (mid July, early August, mid August). Significant differences noted with '*'.

Table 1. *To be included.*

Observer Variability and Accuracy in Estimating Perpendicular and Radial Distances

Methods.---We compared the direct perpendicular distance estimates of three simultaneous observers on n = 113 targets under typical survey conditions (see above) over several weeks to assess variability. Most of the targets were marbled murrelets; remaining targets were other seabirds. Observers looked at the same target at the same time and recorded their distance estimates independently. Data were analyzed with two ANOVAs, one using observer as the factor and one using observer, sea condition, and the interaction of observer and sea condition as factors. Sea condition was defined as wave height less than or greater than 12 cm. Data also were compared with paired *t*-tests.

We tested the accuracy of distance estimates using three other observers and running random line transects through an array of stationary targets (small, anchored buoys). We compared, with paired *t*-tests, each observer's estimate of radial distance with the actual radial distance as measured with a laser rangefinder at the same time and from the same observation point. We also compared, with paired *t*-tests, each observer's direct estimate of perpendicular distance to the perpendicular distance calculated from the laser-measured radial distance and the angle obtained from the bearings recorded by the radial distance observer. Two bearings were read from a digital compass for each target: the bearing of the transect line, and the bearing of the target. Difference between these measures was the angle of the target from the transect line. Perpendicular distance was calculated as:

perpendicular distance = absolute value(radial distance * sin(angle of target from line))

Each observer was not estimating both radial and perpendicular distances at each target. For a given number of targets, each observer was assigned one method and continued to use that method until a sample of ~40 had been recorded. Observers then changed to a different method for the next 40+ targets.

Results.---Of the three observers simultaneously estimating perpendicular distance to the same target, one observer consistently had a higher estimate than the other two. This was not a significant difference when just observer was considered in ANOVA models ($F = 0.648$, $p = 0.52$; Figure 5). In paired *t*-tests, distances of this observer were significantly greater compared to one of the other observers, by 5 meters on average (Table 2). Differences between other pairs of observers were 1.5 and 2.75 m, on average, per target. Sea condition affected distance estimates for two of the three observers ($F = 5.18$, $p = 0.02$; Figure 5), with lower average distances at wave heights > 12 cm compared with < 12 cm.

When directly compared with a known distance, observers under- and overestimated radial distances, with average mean differences ranging 0.4 - 9.6 m (Figure 6). All three observers overestimated perpendicular distance when compared to a perpendicular distance calculated from the laser-measured radial distance. Direct estimates were on average 5.4 - 22 m greater than laser-based calculated distances (Figure 7).

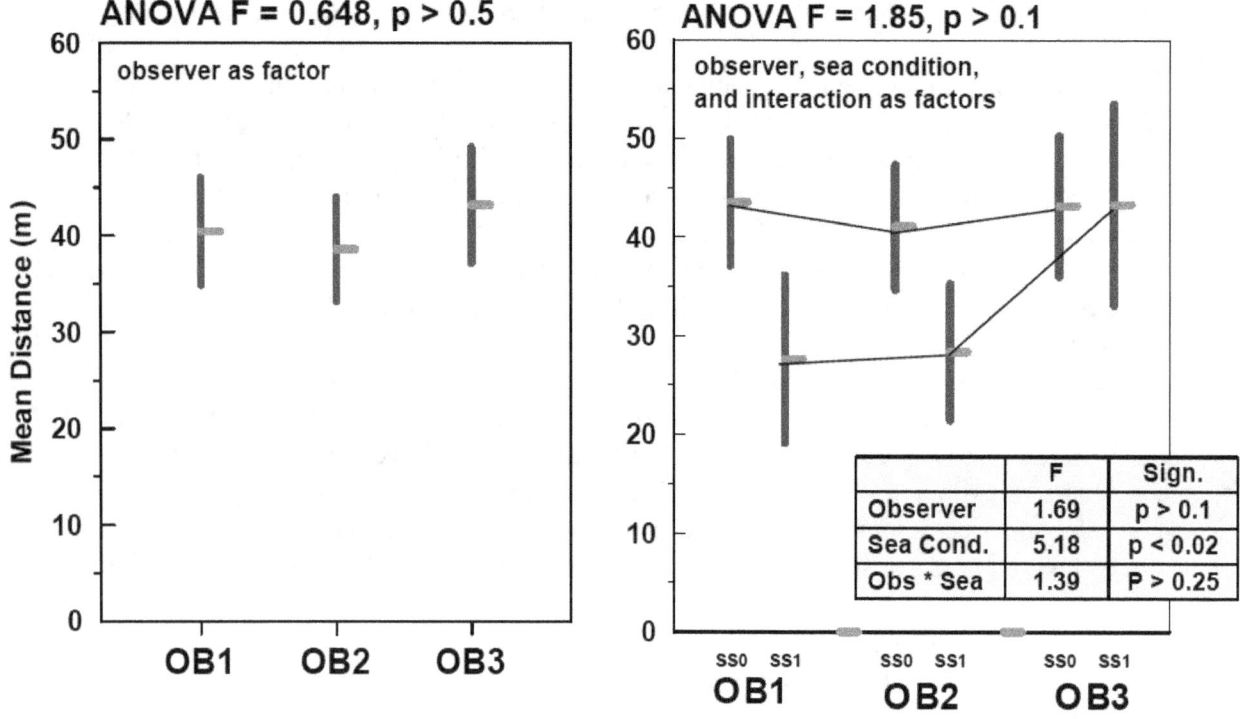

Figure 5. Comparison of mean estimated perpendicular distances among three simultaneous observers and under two sea conditions.

Table 2. Differences in direct perpendicular estimates between pairs of simultaneous observers.

Observer	Mean Distance (n)	95% CI	Observer Pair	Mean Difference (n)	t	Sig.
Obs1	38.24 (130)	33.5-43.0				
Obs2	39.73 (130)	34.8-44.7				
Obs3	43.20 (113)	37.1-49.3				
			1-2	-1.49 (130)	-1.32	0.19
			1-3	-4.60 (113)	-3.79	0.00
			3-2	2.75 (113)	1.67	0.98

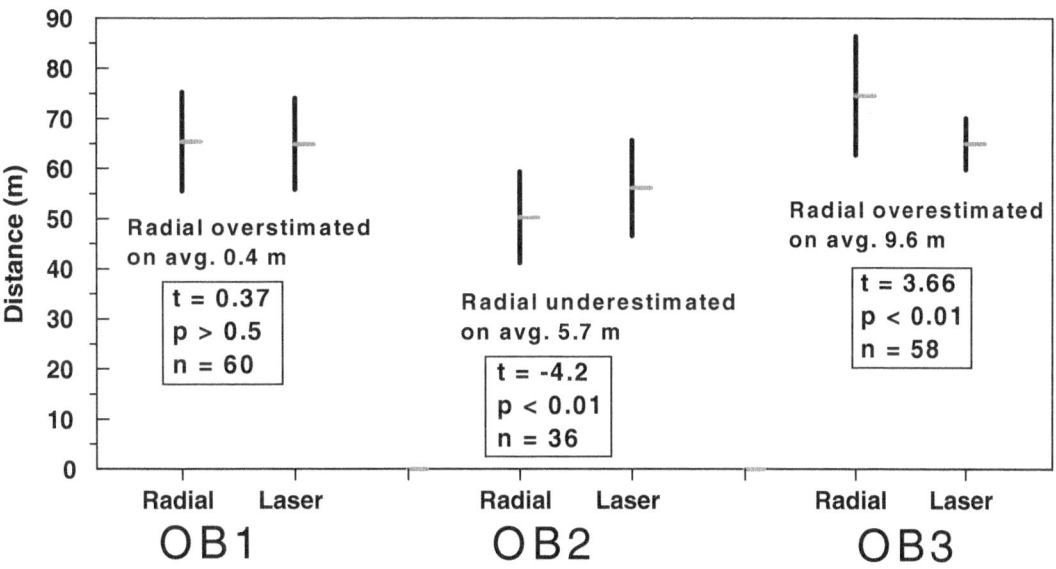

Figure 6.   Performance of individual observers in estimating radial distances, as tested against a laser rangefinder.

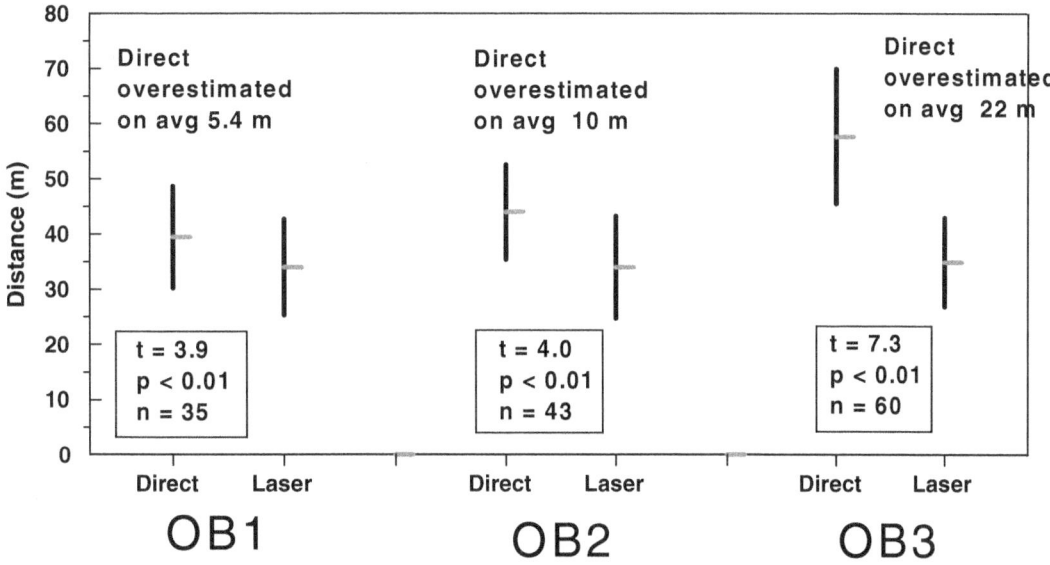

Figure 7. Comparison of observers' direct estimates of perpendicular distance with a perpendicular distance calculated from laser rangefinder-measured radial distances and angles.

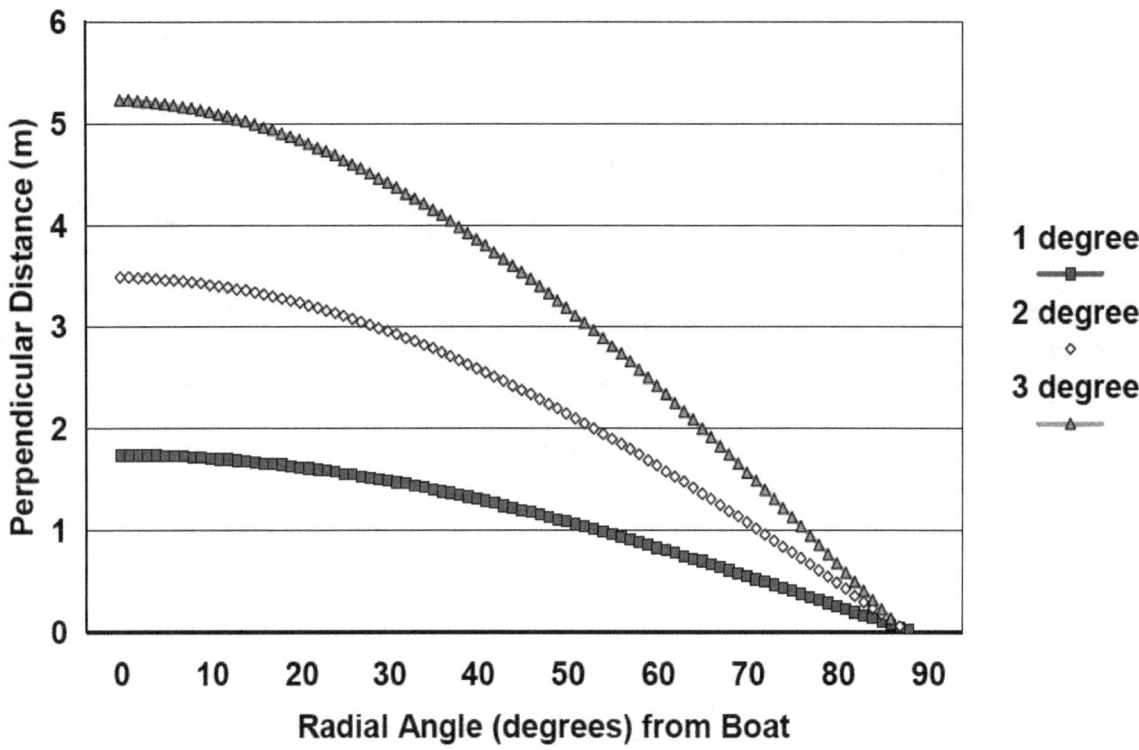

Figure 8. Effect of angle errors on calculated perpendicular distance at a radial distance of 100 m.

Discussion.---Most survey teams deploy a line from the stern of the boat and move the line in and out to calibrate observers to different straight-line distances. Observers receive instant feedback on the accuracy of their estimate. However, objects on the water in front of the boat appear in a different perspective, and distances may be more difficult to gauge. This is particularly true if trying to translate to perpendicular distance. By using a rangefinder, it is possible to apply the same training to direct perpendicular estimates that are used for straight-line estimates. Evaluating the variability among observers' distance estimates early on allows for sufficient training to reduce that variability. In addition, consistent over- or underestimates can be accounted for in data analysis by applying a correction factor.

We used laser-measured distance to calculate the 'true' perpendicular distance in one experiment. However, this calculation is equally dependent on the angle of the target from the line. Our comparison of perpendicular to radial estimates was not completely controlled in that the boat may have drifted off course between the time that the observer estimating perpendicular distance recorded her/his estimate and the observer with the compass obtained two bearings. This did occur, especially early on in the experiment, but the extent to which this may have affected results is unknown. In addition, the compasses on occasion gave inconsistent readings from the same point. This was not quantified during the experiment, but subsequent tests of the compass showed a consistent 2-3^0 difference in repeated readings. Differences ('error') of 1-2^0 would not have a great influence on the perpendicular distance, but larger errors, particularly if the boat moved between one method and the other, could explain differences in direct vs. calculated perpendicular estimates (Figure 8). An improved design would be to obtain a laser-measured perpendicular distance to use as the reference distance from the line, eliminating the angle calculation in establishing the 'true' distance.

Direct Perpendicular vs. Radial Distance-based Density Estimates – Experiment I

Methods.--We established random line transects through an array of stationary targets (small, anchored buoys). When a target was selected, the boat was slowed or stopped. One observer directly estimated perpendicular distance from the transect line, a second observer estimated the radial distance and recorded compass bearings of the transect line and the target, and the third observer measured the radial distance with a laser rangefinder at the same time and from the same observation point as the observer estimating radial distance. We then computed three perpendicular distances for each target: the direct estimate, the distance calculated from the estimated radial distance and angle, and the distance calculated from the laser-measured radial distance and angle (see above). Pooling across three observers, we compared density estimates derived from the program DISTANCE (Buckland et al. 1993) for the three methods. For the DISTANCE program, we established an arbitrary transect length of 10 km, used all targets as one sample per method, and proportioned observations into 1 of 6 distance bands as described above.

We also compared methods under real survey conditions using two simultaneous observers. One observer conducted a typical extensive survey, estimating perpendicular distance to all murrelet and nonmurrelet targets. The second observer worked independently, estimating radial distances and obtaining compass bearings for murrelet targets only. Unlike the experiment with the stationary array, it was not intended that observers recorded the same target at the same time, or even observed the same targets. The second observer was positioned behind the first observer to minimize the chances of cuing each other to birds. We conducted this experiment on 14 transects ranging from 2-36 km in length. We compared numbers of murrelets detected per transect with paired *t*-tests, and compared density estimates (from program DISTANCE) derived from pooling across transects.

Results.--- Density estimates from the perpendicular distances derived from the three methods used in the stationary array were based on 143 targets pooled across observers. The density based on direct estimates of radial distance was highest, the density based on laser-measured radial distance was slightly lower, and the density from the direct estimate of perpendicular distance was lowest (Figure 9).

Under real survey situations, the observer estimating radial distances and taking compass bearings recorded fewer murrelets than the observer estimating perpendicular distance. The difference was not significant across all transects, averaging 12 fewer murrelets per transect ($t =$ 1.467, $p = 0.163$). However, looking at transects individually suggested that the differences occurred when the encounter rate of murrelets was higher and sustained, exceeding 20 birds/km for a number of km (Table 3). Despite differences in the number of murrelets detected, density estimates were similar between the two methods (Figure 10). The numbers of murrelets and murrelet groups (not weighted by number in the group) recorded within 50 m of the transect line were similar between methods (Figures 11 and 12). Observers estimating radial distances recorded significantly fewer murrelets than expected at distances > 75 m from the transect line ($X^2 = 6.0$, $p < 0.02$ in each case; Figure 11), but these had little influence on density estimates.

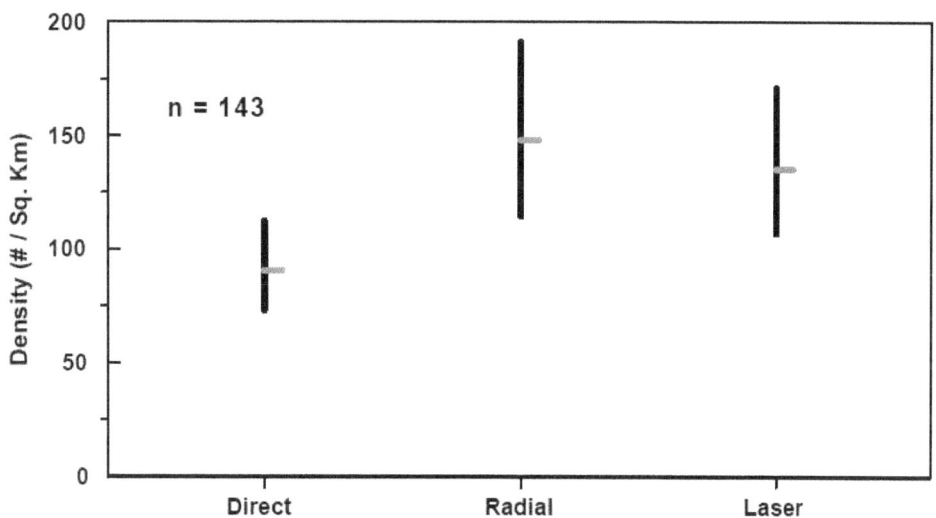

Figure 9. Density estimates (from program DISTANCE) and 95% confidence intervals from three methods of obtaining perpendicular distances: direct estimates, calculated from estimates of radial distance and measured angles, and calculated from laser-measured radial distance and measured angles.

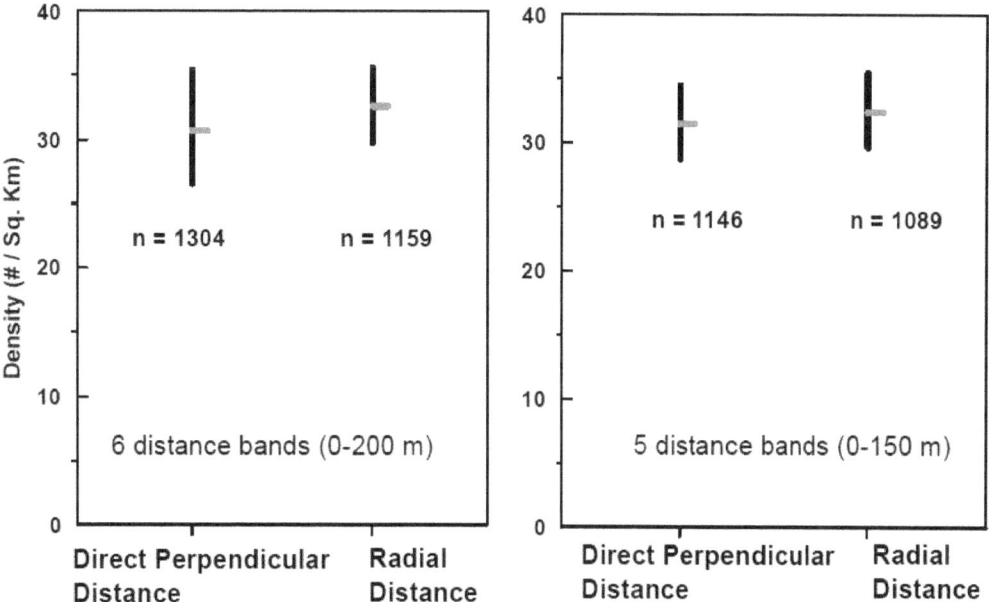

Figure 10. Comparison of density estimates based on perpendicular and radial distance estimates obtained under real survey conditions.

Table 3. Comparison by transect of the number of murrelets detected using perpendicular distance method and the radial distance and angle method. Table is organized by increasing encounter rate (no. murrelets/km).

Date	Transect	Km	Perpendicular Method		Radial Method	
			Total MM	No./km	Total MM	No./km
8/27/98	ORES	36	25	0.7	24	0.7
8/20/98	LOSE	8	7	0.9	5	0.6
8/20/98	DECA	22	49	2.2	46	2.1
8/24/98	WALD	16	48	3.0	46	2.9
8/21/98	LOSO	10	33	3.3	34	3.4
8/24/98	ORWE	14	55	3.9	51	3.6
7/28/98	LOSO	10	54	5.4	52	5.2
8/27/98	CYPR	22	118	5.4	110	5.0
8/25/98	ORSW	4	22	5.5	24	6.0
8/27/98	CONE	2	11	5.5	12	6.0
8/25/98	WASP	6	47	7.8	45	7.5
8/25/98	JONE	6	49	8.2	51	8.5
8/21/98	LOSW	14	214	15.3	218	15.6
8/10/98	SJNO	10	239[a]	23.9	160[a]	16.0
8/24/98	SJNO	12	339[a]	28.2	230[a]	19.2
8/25/98	CRAN	4	147[b]	36.7	157[b]	39.2

[a] Greatest differences in number of murrelets between methods. Encounter rate > 20 birds/km.
[b] High encounter rate, but numbers of birds similar. Length of transect short.

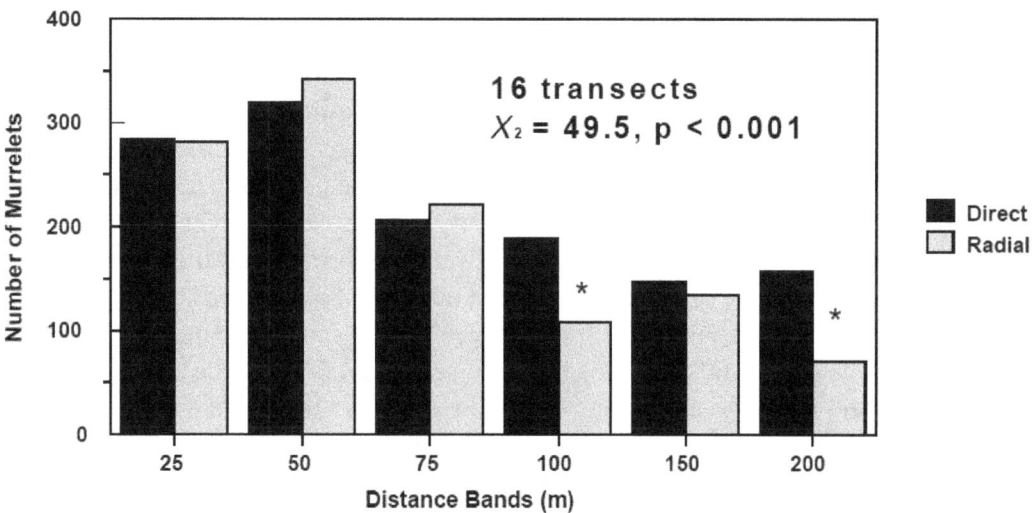

Figure 11. Distribution of murrelets from the transect line as detected by observers conducting simultaneous but independent surveys using two methods of obtaining perpendicular distance. Significant differences noted with '*'.

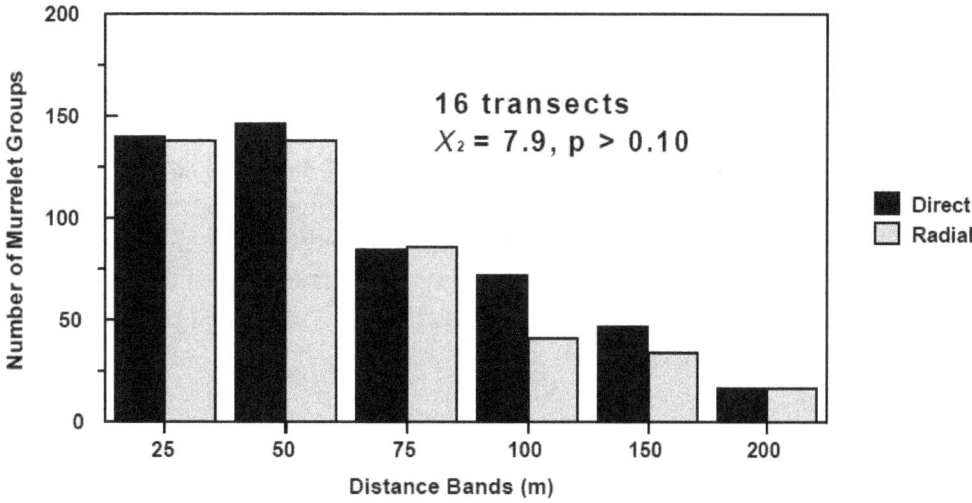

Figure 12. Distribution of murrelet groups (not weighted by the number in a group) from the transect line as detected by observers conducting simultaneous but independent surveys using two methods of obtaining perpendicular distance.

Discussion.— Based on density estimates alone, the results from the experiment conducted under real survey conditions suggest that it makes little difference if observers estimate perpendicular distances or estimate radial distances and take compass bearings. However, if the actual number of murrelets recorded is critical, the results suggest that using the compass to obtain two bearings per target may cause the observer to miss birds in high-density areas. (The differences can't really be explained by observer variability.) The observer with the compass should have had an advantage in that she/he was only recording murrelets, while the other observer was recording all species. This should be considered in terms of the additional information (other than density estimates) that is obtained from survey data, such as the number of adults and juveniles to compute age ratios. It may be proposed that 'interference' of the compass could be minimized by estimating angles as well as distances. This has two weaknesses. First, the error associated with estimates of any kind would be compounded. One reason that the radial method has been supported is that it may be easier to estimate a radial distance than a perpendicular distance because a radial distance is equivalent to a direct line of sight. Combined with an angle that is accurately measured, the calculated perpendicular distance could be more accurate. However, if the accuracy of the angle is reduced, the benefit of using this method becomes questionable. Secondly, the magnitude of errors in angle measures would likely increase if observers were estimating rather than measuring them. What was a 1-2^0 error in the compass itself could become much greater, with a greater error associated with the calculated perpendicular distance. This would most affect targets closer to the transect line (extrapolate from Figure 8), which are the more critical for density estimates with the program DISTANCE. The potential impact of angle estimation error should be tested before estimates of angles are considered as part of the survey methodology.

The density derived from direct perpendicular distance estimates was lower than the density derived from a known radial distance (the experiment with a fixed array). As discussed on pg. 10, this comparison was weakened by the use of a calculated perpendicular distance as a reference point, rather than a measured perpendicular distance. This result also may reflect observers' tendency to overestimate perpendicular distances. This could have a subtle effect on how numbers of murrelets are assigned to distance classes within the DISTANCE program, affecting the density estimate. The density derived from radial distance estimates was higher than that from the known radial distance, although not significantly so. From a conservation standpoint, one might consider whether an underestimate or overestimate of density is more prudent. Again, the degree to which these methods actually differ can't be conclusively determined until tests with improved controls are conducted.

Direct Perpendicular vs. Radial Distance-based Density Estimates – Experiment II

Methods.–We deployed a sample of 36 buoys (3.8 l plastic milk jugs) tied to 0.23-kg (8-oz) weights in waters of southern Puget Sound where water depth averaged about 6 m. Buoys were spaced at random intervals throughout a rectangular area approximately 0.5 km wide and 10 km long. We used two boats to run transect lines through the array of buoys. Multiple passes were made from various angles to obtain a larger sample of distance estimates. Each boat was staffed by 3 people; two experienced observers made distance estimates and the other person piloted the boat. Prior to collecting observations, a 100-m line with visible markers at 25-m intervals was trailed behind each boat to help calibrate distance estimates. For a set of observations, usually about 40, one observer directly estimated the perpendicular distance between a buoy and the transect line. The other observer made an estimate of the radial distance from the boat to the target and used a digital compass to record the azimuth of the transect and the azimuth to the target. When the boat progressed to a point where the target was abeam (along a perpendicular line from the transect) one observer (the one doing the direct perpendicular estimate) measured the actual perpendicular distance to the target using a laser rangefinder. The maximum range of the instrument was about 70 m under the conditions of our tests. The boat operator made a concerted effort to keep the boat on the established course and to account for water current 'set' to minimize errors introduced by changes in the boat's position between the time an observer made an estimate and the boat became abeam of the target. Current did create some problems, as evident from the relative change in buoy position for those that were originally estimated far in front of the boat, but we do not feel this was a serious problem. After completing a set of observations, the observers switched roles. This cycle was repeated over 1.5 days, 14-15 January 1999. Weather conditions varied from calm to breezy with overcast skies or light rain. Waves were flat to moderate (sea state 0 to 1). For the radial estimates, perpendicular distance (x) was calculated as $x = \sin(\theta) \cdot r$ where θ was the angular deviation from the transect line to the target and r was the radial distance from the observer to the target. Angular deviation was calculated as the difference in azimuths of the transect line and the target.

To compare direct and radial estimates of perpendicular distance with actual distance, we computed a regression with actual distance as the independent variable and the estimate as dependent variable. We also computed the difference between each estimate and the actual distance and compared mean differences using matched-pair t-test. We also grouped the data into distance intervals of 0-25, 25-50, 50-75, 75-100, and 100-125 m and used program DISTANCE to compute detectability functions and density of the buoys for each method. We assumed a total transect length of 100 km for density calculations. The density estimates were pooled across observers and all observations for one method were entered into the program as a single sample.

Results.–We obtained a total of 321 observations; because of missing data in each method, the total sample with complete data was 305. For the radial estimate, a regression of the estimate (y) on the actual measured distance (x) was $y = 0.80x + 4.71$; $R^2 = 0.68$; SE y|x = 10.27 (Figure 13). For the direct estimate, the regression was $y = 0.89x + 5.52$; $R^2 = 0.78$; SE y|x = 8.67 (Figure 14).

These regression results indicate that the direct estimate was slightly less biased at greater distances than the radial estimate (slope was closer to 1.0) and that the direct estimate was more precise (lower SE y|x, a measure of the variability of the estimates). However, the intercept was greater for the direct estimate, indicating a tendency to overestimate distances to closer targets.

Results of matched-pair t-tests differed from the regression in that the mean difference between radial and measured perpendicular distance did not differ from 0 (mean difference = 0.87 m, t = 1.40, df = 304, P = 0.164), whereas the mean difference did differ from 0 between the direct and measured estimates (mean difference = 2.44 m, t = 4.80, df = 305, P = 0.000). Thus, this test indicated that the direct estimate was more biased than the radial estimate but the amount of bias was small relative to the precision of the distance estimates.

We computed the absolute value of differences between the measured distance and each of the two estimates and computed the mean of these absolute differences. For the direct estimate, the mean of the absolute difference was 6.7 m. For the radial estimate, the mean difference was 8.0 m, indicating, as in the regression results, that the direct estimates were more precise than the radial estimates (matched pair t-test, t = 2.79, df = 304, P = 0.006). For the direct estimate, 28% of our estimates were within 10% of the actual measured perpendicular distance compared to 21% for the radial estimates. We also computed the absolute difference between each estimate and the actual distance expressed as a percent of the actual distance. The mean difference for the direct estimate was 37% (median = 21%); mean difference for the radial estimate was 51% (median = 25%). These results indicate that the direct estimate performed somewhat better than the radial estimate, but both are relatively imprecise.

Results varied among the four observers (Figure 15). Numbers of observations for each of the 4 observers varied from 69 to 84. Using the radial method, 2 observers had mean differences between their estimates and the actual distance that did not differ from 0; one observer overestimated and one observer underestimated the true distance. Using the direct method, the estimates of two observers also included 0, and two observers significantly underestimated the true distance.

We grouped the perpendicular distances into four distance bands under each method (Figure 16) and submitted these grouped data to program DISTANCE to compute detectability functions and density estimates based on each of the three datasets (actual, direct, radial), we found little difference between methods (Figure 17). The detectability function based on actual perpendicular distances was intermediate between the higher radial-based function and the lower direct-based function but confidence intervals overlapped among all estimates. Similarly, the computed density estimate based on the actual distances was intermediate between the higher density from the radial estimate and the lower density from the direct estimate and all confidence intervals overlapped. These results parallel those from our other experiments (see above).

Discussion.–Although the direct estimates performed better in most of the tests we conducted (8 of 10 comparisons), the differences were not strong. We found that the direct estimate was somewhat more precise than the radial method, but that both estimates were biased. Because the differences were slight, we conclude that either method could be used for surveys using the protocols we employed. However, if observers estimate azimuths, radial estimates will have greater error. We used a digital compass to make relatively precise measurements; visual estimates of azimuths, or estimates using angle boards marked at 5-degree intervals will lead to greater error in the radial method.

Neither method is as accurate as we would prefer. As noted above, the average difference between the actual perpendicular distance and the estimated distance was 8.0 m for the radial estimate (51% error) and 6.7 m for the direct estimate (37% error). Only about a quarter of all observations fell within plus or minus 10% of the actual distance under either method.

We are concerned about other problems using the radial method, as discussed in Experiment I. Because more time is needed to collect radial distances and azimuths, there is a risk of missing birds. Our results, for example, suggest that observers missed birds significant numbers of murrelets using the radial method compared with the direct method (Table 3) on one transect with high numbers of encounters. On transects with lower numbers of encounters, numbers of birds were very similar for the two methods.

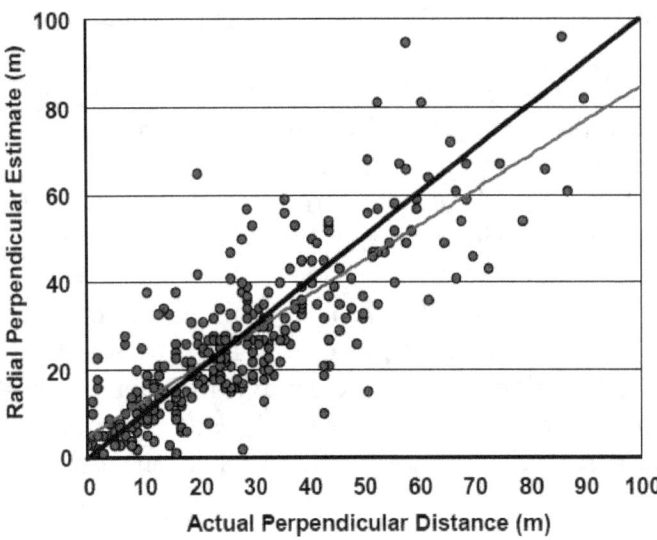

Figure 13. Relationship between actual perpendicular distance to fixed buoys (measured with laser rangefinder) and distance estimated using radial distance and angle. Heavy line indicates equal estimates (slope = 1.0); thinner line is regression between actual and radial estimates.

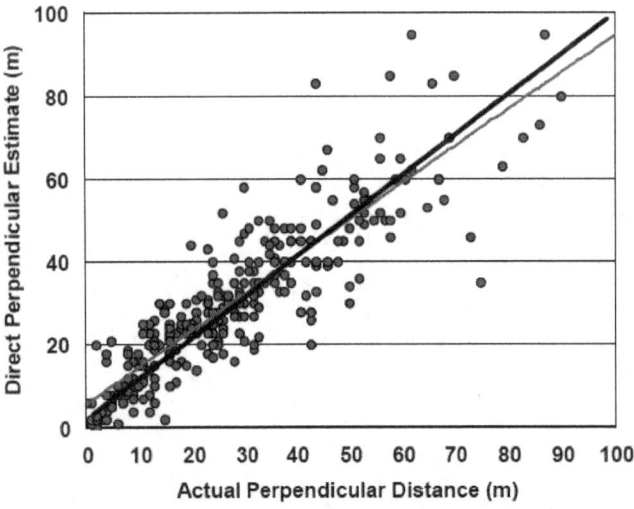

Figure 14. Relationship between actual perpendicular distance to fixed buoys (measured with laser rangefinder) and direct estimate of perpendicular distance. Heavy line indicates equal estimates (slope = 1.0); thinner line is regression between actual and direct estimates.

Direct Estimate

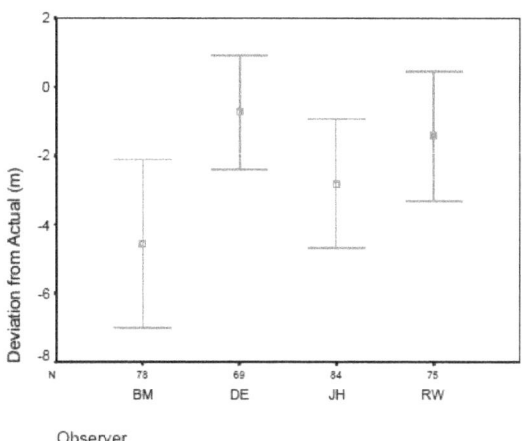

Radial Estimate

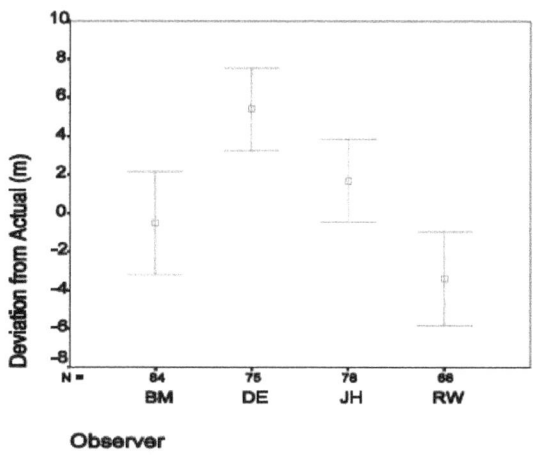

Figure 15. Variation among observers in difference between estimated and actual perpendicular distances to buoys using direct (top) and radial (bottom) estimation technique. Values are mean and 95% confidence intervals.

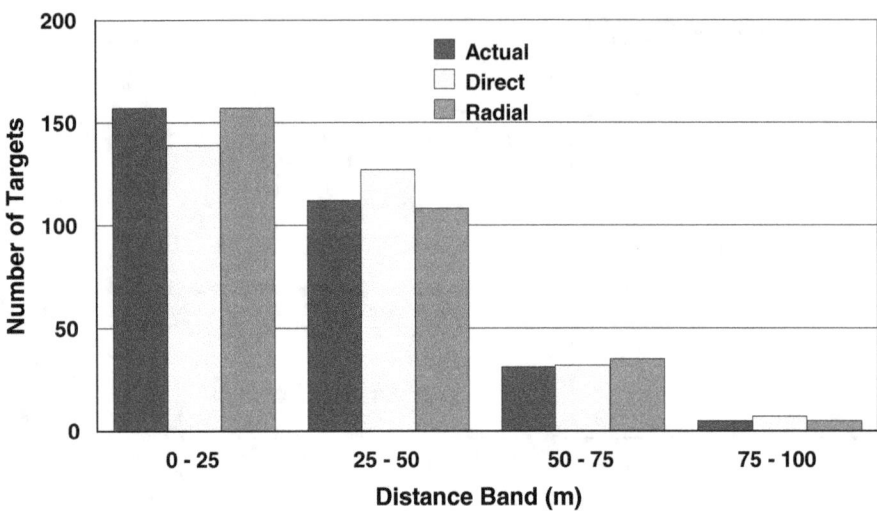

Figure 16.
Number of buoys observed in four perpendicular distance classes using three techniques. Actual = perpendicular distance from the boat to a buoy measured using a laser rangefinder; Direct = perpendicular distance between the projected transect line and a bouy as visually estimated by an observer; Radial = perpendicular distance calculated from an observer's estimate of radial distance to the buoy and the angle between the transect line and the buoy. These grouped distance data were used as input to program DISTANCE to compute detectability functions and density estimates for each method.

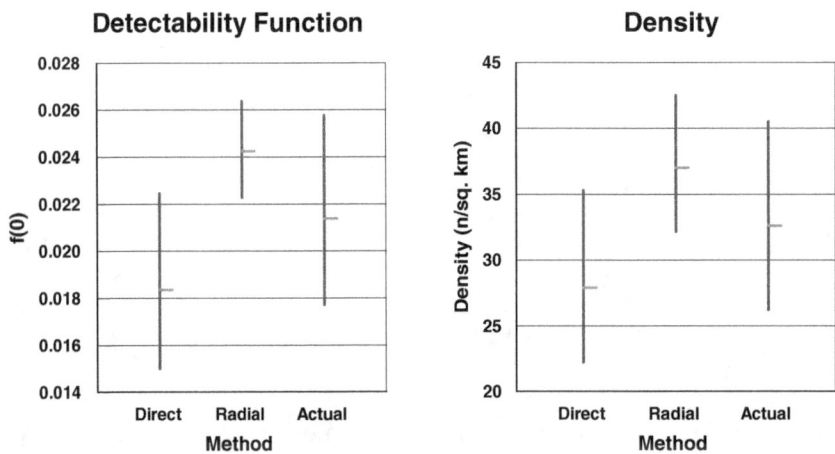

Figure 17. Detectability and density of buoys from 3 measures of perpendicular distance. Direct = direct estimate of perpendicular distance between target and transect line; radial = perpendicular distance calculated from estimate of radial distance between observer and target and angle between transect line and target; Actual = perpendicular distance between observer and target as measured with a laser rangefinder. Detectability and density were calculated using program distance assuming 100 km of transect. Sample size was 305 targets in each case.

Observer Variability in Identifying Adult and Juvenile Marbled Murrelets

Methods.----We compared the classification of marbled murrelets by three simultaneous observers on n = 102 murrelet groups under typical survey conditions (see above) over several weeks during July and August 1998 to assess variability. Observers looked at the same groups at the same time and recorded each murrelet as 1 of 11 possible age classes adapted from Strong 1995. Each of 5 classes could be recorded as definite or probable, with the 11th class being 'unknown'. Comparisons were made of the total numbers per class and of the juvenile:adult ratios calculated from the data.   Adults were defined as definite class 1+2+ 3 + probable class 1+2+3. Juveniles were defined as definite + probable class 5. Unknowns were class 11. Class 4 birds were not included in calculations, as by definition these are birds in basic plumage that could be fully-molted adults or juveniles. In this experiment, no birds were classified as class 4 because questionable birds were examined until a determination of adult or juvenile could be made, or they were classed as unknown.

Results.—There were differences in how observers classed murrelets, but none of these affected the total number of adults recorded (Table 4). Total number of adults differed by < 3%. The sample of juveniles was much smaller, where differences of 1-2 birds could be important. Observer 1 recorded the fewest juveniles and the most adults, yielding the lowest juvenile:adult ratio. However, all of the ratios were well below the level needed for population stability if survivorship is assumed to be 0.85 (Beissinger 1995).   Thus, all three ratios would have led to the same conclusion about population status.

Discussion.—The variability we observed was generally minimal, although one observer may have misidentified 1-2 juveniles as adults. One would expect that if confusion was to occur, it would be with advanced-molt birds. In this sample, all three observers had very similar numbers of definite class 3 birds and no probable class 3's, so it appears that this isn't the source of the difference in numbers of juveniles. Variability in classification among observers likely could be reduced with more orientation to plumage classes, more training by actual observations, and with better understanding of when to classify a bird as definite, probable, or unknown.

Table 4. Classification of marbled murrelets by three simultaneous observers.

	OB1	OB2	OB3
Class 1 - Definite	152	133	141
Class 1 - Probable	4	10	0
Class 2 - Definite	38	45	46
Class 2 - Probable	1	0	9
Class 3 - Definite	21	22	19
Class 3 - Probable	0	0	0
Total Adult	216	210	215
Class 4 - Definite	0	0	0
Class 4 - Probable	0	0	0
Class 5 - Definite	7	10	9
Class 5 - Probable	0	0	0
Total Juvenile	7	10	9
Unknown	6	13	6
Juv:Ad Ratio	0.032	0.048	0.042

Differences in Spatial Distribution and Detectability of Adult and Juvenile Murrelets

Methods.—To assess detectability, we compiled data from 16 line transects totaling 170 km that were repeated every 10 days from early June - late August in 1997 and 1998. Transects were 300 m from shore. We compared the probability density function from the program DISTANCE of adults to that of juveniles for the 10-day intervals in which juveniles were present. Density functions were based on direct estimates of perpendicular distance from the transect line. Distances were assigned to one of six bands: 0-25 m from the line, 0-25 m, 25-50 m, 50-75 m, 75-100 m, 100-150 m, and 150-200 m.

To compare distributions, we combined extensive and intensive survey data from the SJI in 1997 and 1998. We computed the actual distance from shore of all known-age murrelets (n = 6724) based on their distance from the transect line, the transects's distance from shore, and the direction of the boat for each transect. All murrelets had been identified as adult, juvenile, or unknown in 1997. For the 1998 data, where murrelets were classified as 1 of 11 classes, we included definite and probable class 1, 2 and 3 murrelets as adults and definite and probable class 5 birds as juveniles. We compared seasonal distribution from shore between years across 6 time intervals from early June - late August. We also investigated the distribution within the SJI by comparing the patterns of peak and low numbers of adults and juveniles at 8 locations across 6 seasons in both years.

Results.—Adults and juveniles were similarly distributed across distance bands from the transect line (Figure 18). Both distributions followed the expected pattern of more birds detected closer to line and fewer as distance from the line increased. As a result, probability density functions were similar (Figure 19), suggesting no difference in the ability to detect adults compared with juveniles based on their distribution around line transects run at 300 m from shore.

Based on actual distance from shore, the distribution of juveniles was skewed slightly closer to shore compared with adults, although the mean difference was not statistically significant. In 1997, juveniles moved closer to shore as the season progressed from late July to late August, whereas adult distribution remained stable (Figure 20). Mean distance from shore for juveniles exceeded 300 m in late July, and decreased to < 250 m by late August. This pattern was repeated somewhat in 1998, but the decrease in mean distance from shore occurred earlier in the summer and did not continue to decrease through the last season. Mean distance from shore of adults generally exceeded 300 m, and exceeded 350 m during late June 1997 (Figure 20).

There were no obvious differences in the patterns of adult and juveniles at 8 locations around the SJI during 1997 (Figure 21). In general, places that showed increases in adults as the summer progressed also had higher numbers of juveniles, and vice versa. In 1998, 4 of the 8 locations showed contrasting patterns. At 2 sites (SJSW and LOSO), juveniles increased as the number of adults decreased. At two other sites (LOSW and WASP), juveniles decreased as the number of adults increased (Figure 21).

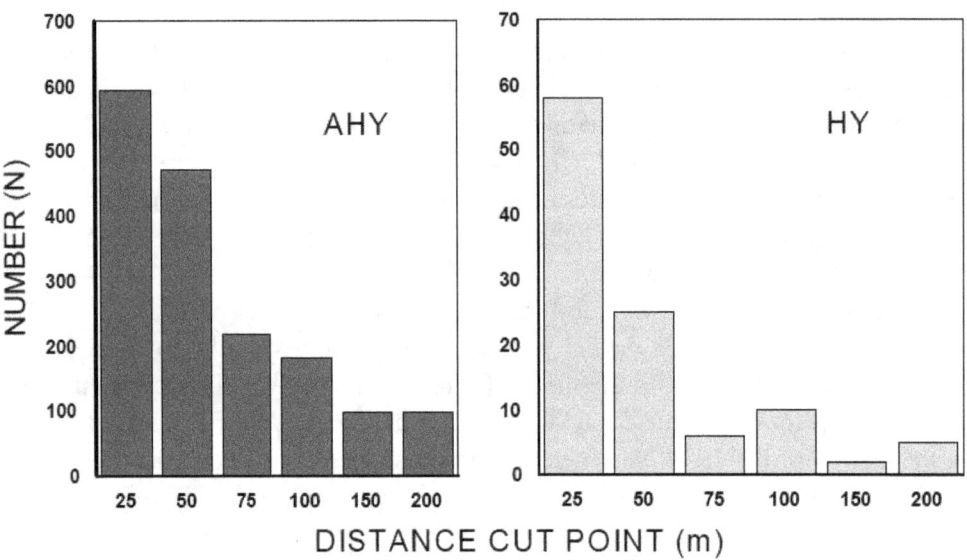

Figure 18. Distribution of adult (AHY) and juvenile (HY) marbled murrelets from the transect line across 16 transects surveyed in each of five time intervals (intervals 5-9) during mid July - late August 1997. Distributions similar for 1998.

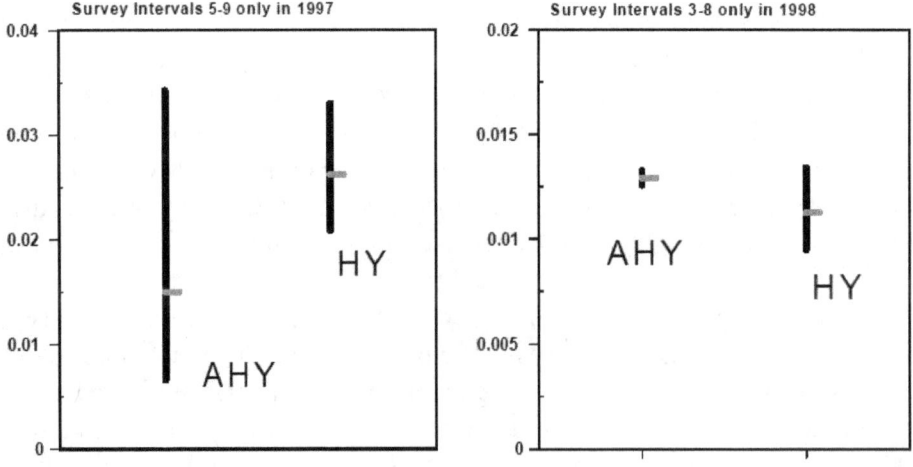

Figure 19. Probability density functions [$f(0)$] for adult (AHY) and juvenile (HY) marbled murrelets during July-August 1997 and 1998.

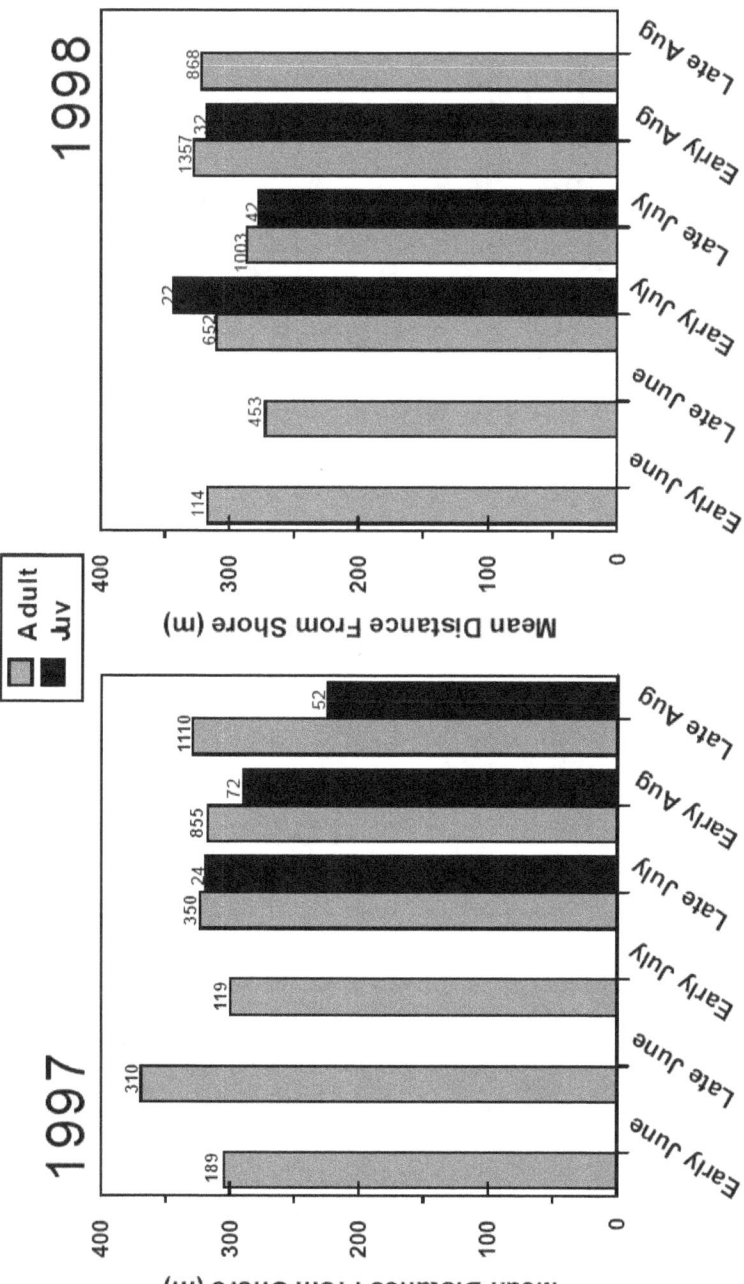

Figure 20. Distribution from shore of adult and juvenile marbled murrelets by season and year. Numbers above bars are numbers of murrelets.

Seasonal Distribution of
Adult and Juvenile Murrelets

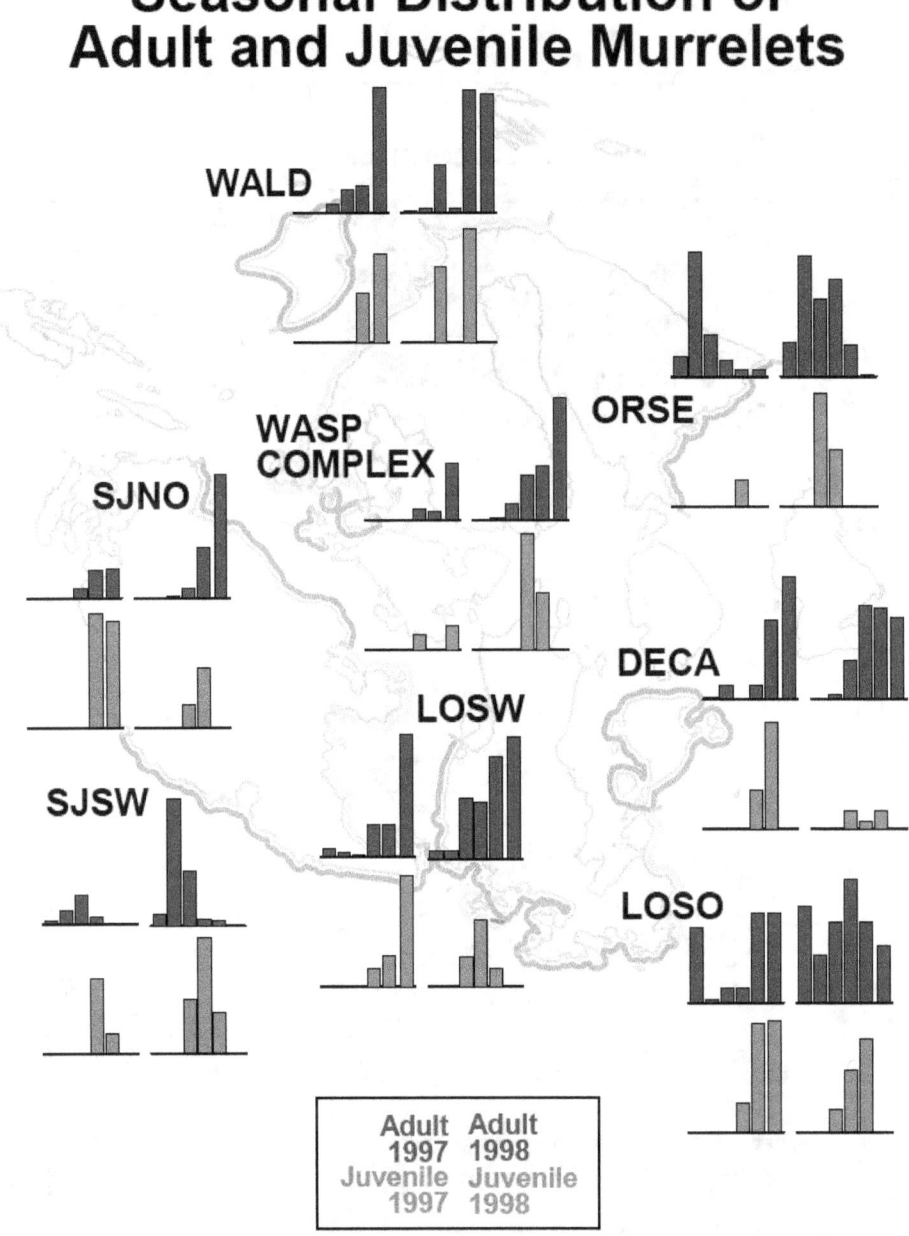

Figure 21. Distribution of numbers of adult and juvenile marbled murrelets within and between seasons at eight locations within the San Juan Island archipelago. Heights of bars are not comparable between locations and between adults and juveniles. Only the patterns (peaks and lows) are comparable for each location. Seasons = 1-15 June, 16-30 June, 1-15 July, 16-31 July, 1-15 Aug, and 16-31 Aug.

Effect of Transect Configuration on Density Estimates

Methods.--- We tested two configurations, a zig zag and rectangular transect, against a 'straight line' configuration (uniform distance from shore) in the SJI in 1997 (Figure 22 -*need*). The straight-line transects were a subset of our established core transects. They followed the contour of the shoreline at a distance of 300 m from shore and were comprised of 2-km segments. We used marine radar to maintain course at this uniform distance. The rectangular configuration began as a core straight-line transect (i.e., on an established line 300 m from shore). The boat traveled parallel to shore along the straight-line transect for 750 m, then turned 90^0 and headed perpendicular from shore to a distance of 700 m (positioning the boat at 1000 m from shore). The boat then turned to continue parallel to shore for a distance of 500 m, then headed straight back to shore for a distance of 700 m back to the 300-m line. The boat then finished the 2-km segment by traveling along the 300-m line for 750 m. Each subsequent 2-km segment was repeated with this same design until the end of the transect had been reached. Distances for each jog were measured with a GPS unit and the distance from shore (300 or 1000 m) confirmed with the radar. The zig zag transect began at the same origin (landmark) as a straight line transect, but at a point 100 m from shore. The line then proceeded at an arbitrary angle away from the shore until a distance of 1000 m from shore had been reached. The line then headed at another arbitrary angle back to shore to a distance of 100 m from shore. This pattern was repeated until the ending point of the core transect was reached. Each leg of the zig zag transect was recorded and stored with a GPS unit so that the 'route' could be recalled from the GPS and repeated. Legs did not equate to 2-km segments. The 100-m and 1000-m distances from shore were determined with marine radar.

For all three methods, observers estimated the perpendicular distance of all murrelet groups up to 200 m either side of the transect line. In addition, the actual distance from shore of each murrelet group was measured by radar for groups encountered when the boat was not traveling parallel to shore at a known distance. A total of 10 transects were run with the three configurations. Straight-line configurations were run first; the transect area was repeated with the zig zag and rectangular pattern either immediately after (n = 4) or the next day (n = 6). The 10 transects were conducted during 3 time intervals: last week of July (n = 4), early-mid August (n = 2), and late August (n = 4). We compared the number of murrelets detected by transect by method, the number detected per km by method and time interval, and the density estimates from program DISTANCE by method for each interval across transects within the interval. For DISTANCE, murrelet groups were assigned to 1 of 6 perpendicular distance classes (0-25 m, 25-50 m, 50-75 m, 75-100 m, 100-150 m, and 150-200 m).

Results.—The zig zag configuration had the lowest number of total murrelets detected, the lowest number per linear km, and the lowest density estimate of the three methods (Figures 23 and 24). Rectangular configurations yielded the highest numbers of birds in 2 of the 3 intervals, but lower numbers/km compared with the straight-line method. Differences in density estimates between the straight line and rectangle may be a sample size problem. The straight-line density estimate was much higher in the interval when only two transects were covered, and the rectangular estimate was higher in the interval when more transects were covered. The zig zag method was similar to the other two methods only in the first interval, when the number of murrelets detected was very low.

Discussion.---The zig zag method spent less time sampling the area where murrelets are more likely to be in the SJI, thus we detected fewer murrelet groups on transects of this configuration. However, this may not be a problem from a monitoring standpoint, when the most appropriate sampling approach may not be to target the highest-density areas (Tim Max and others, pers. comm.). The zig zag method has the benefit of covering a range of distances from shore, and may be a good way to cover large expanses of relatively shallow water where murrelets are more evenly distributed away from shore (i.e., bays or coves). The rectangular configuration is more similar to a typical extensive survey in that it spends most of its time running parallel to shore at an 'optimum' distance, but also forays out to a greater distance as a spot check of the distribution of murrelets further from shore. Our design did not incorporate a line heading toward shore, because at 300 m from shore and with a transect width of 200 m either side of the line, we were essentially sampling from 100 m from shore. The rectangular configuration may be prone to double counting near the junctions of the perpendicular lines (leaving and returning to the line parallel to shore), especially if the transect width is large (i.e., 200 m either side of the boat, as in this case).

On more than half of the samples, the straight-line method was run a day before the rectangular and zigzag methods. Even when all methods were run in succession on the same day, the time lapsed from one method to the next is certainly enough for birds to move into or out of the sampling area, especially if the transect is 8-10 km long. This lack of simultaneous observations limits these comparisons to that extent. The only way to remove this confounding factor under field conditions would be to run three boats at the same time.

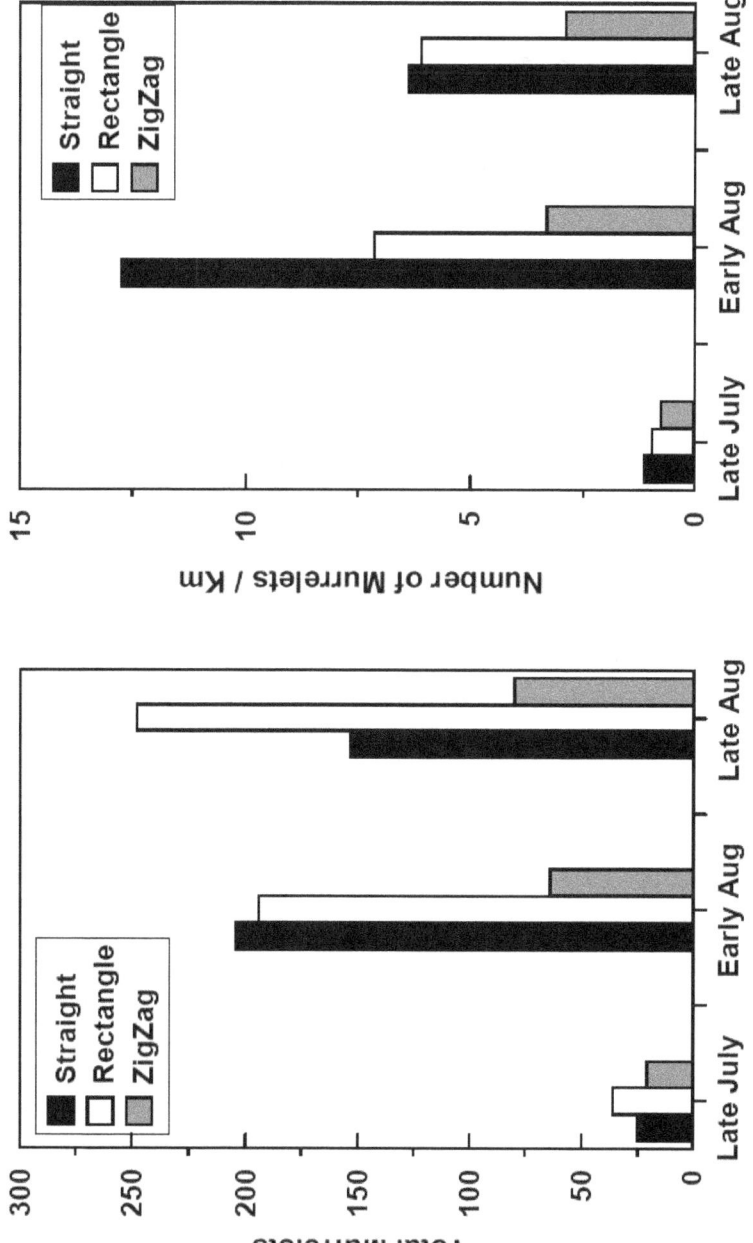

Figure 23. Comparison of the total number of murrelets and the number per linear km detected on three transect configurations during three time intervals in the San Juan Islands in 1997.

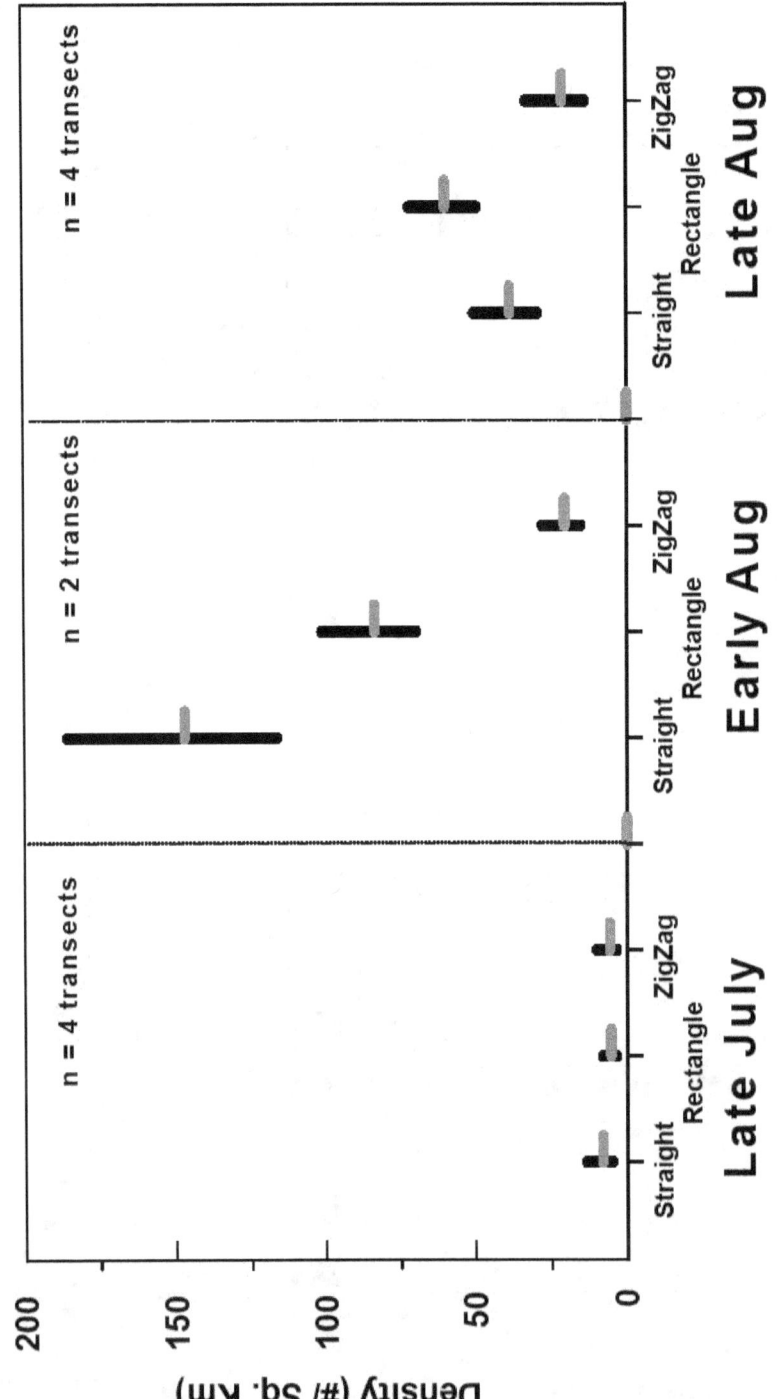

Figure 24. Marbled murrelet density estimates (program DISTANCE) for each of three transect configurations for three time intervals in the San Juan Islands, 1997. Densities estimated using transects within an interval as the sample.

Literature Cited

Beissinger, S.R. 1995. Population trends of the marbled murrelet projected from demographic analyses. P. 385-393 *In* Ralph, C.J., G.L. Hunt, Jr., M.G. Raphael, and J.F. Piatt, eds. Ecology and conservation of the marbled murrelet. Gen. Tech. Rep. PSW-152. Albany, CA: U.S. Department of Agriculture, Forest Service, Pacific Southwest Research Station.

Buckland, S.T., D.R. Anderson, K.P. Burnham, and J.L. Laake. 1993. Distance sampling: estimating abundance of biological populations. New York: Chapman and Hall.

Cooke, F. 1998. Marbled murrelet studies at Desolation Sound, British Columbia. Abstract. P. 33 *In* Pacific Seabird Group 25th Annual Meeting, 21-25 January 1998, Monterey, CA.

Hamer, T.E., and S.K. Nelson. 1995. Characteristics of marbled murrelet nest trees and nesting stands. P. 69-82 *In* Ralph, C.J., G.L. Hunt, Jr., M.G. Raphael, and J.F. Piatt, eds. Ecology and conservation of the marbled murrelet. Gen. Tech. Rep. PSW-152. Albany, CA: U.S. Department of Agriculture, Forest Service, Pacific Southwest Research Station.

Madsen, S., D. Evans, T. Hamer, P. Hensen, S. Miller, S. K. Nelson, D. Roby, and M. Stapanian. 1997. Marbled murrelet effectiveness monitoring plan for the Northwest forest plan. Interim report to the USDA/USDI IAC and REIC. 55 pp.

Nelson, S. K., and T.E. Hamer. 1995. Nesting biology and behavior of the marbled murrelet. P. 57-67 *In* Ralph, C.J., G.L. Hunt, Jr., M.G. Raphael, and J.F. Piatt, eds. Ecology and conservation of the marbled murrelet. Gen. Tech. Rep. PSW-152. Albany, CA: U.S. Department of Agriculture, Forest Service, Pacific Southwest Research Station.

Raphael, M.G. and D.M. Evans. 1997. An evaluation of alternative techniques for estimating productivity of the marbled murrelet, Puget Sound, Washington. Report to the U.S. Fish and Wildlife Service, December 15, 1997.

U.S. Department of Agriculture and Department of the Interior (USDA/USDI). 1994. Record of decision for amendments to Forest Service and Bureau of Land Management planning documents within the range of the Northern Spotted Owl. Portland, OR: Forest Service, Bureau of Land Management.

U.S. Department of the Interior, Fish and Wildlife Service. 1997. Recovery plan for the marbled murrelet (*Brachyrhamphus marmoratus*) in Washington, Oregon, and California. Portland, OR.